LITTLE

Restorative
Teaching Tools

FOR ONLINE LEARNING

Published titles include:

The Little Book of Restorative Justice: Revised & Updated, by Howard Zehr

The Little Book of Conflict Transformation, by John Paul Lederach

The Little Book of Family Group Conferences, New-Zealand Style,
by Allan MacRae and Howard Zehr

The Little Book of Strategic Peacebuilding, by Lisa Schirch

The Little Book of Strategic Negotiation, by Jayne Seminare Docherty

The Little Book of Circle Processes, by Kay Pranis

The Little Book of Contemplative Photography, by Howard Zehr

Little Book of Healthy Organizations, by David Brubaker and Ruth Hoover Zimmerman

The Little Book of Restorative Discipline for Schools, by Lorraine Stutzman Amstutz
and Judy H. Mullet

The Little Book of Trauma Healing, by Carolyn Yoder

The Little Book of Biblical Justice, by Chris Marshall

The Little Book of Restorative Justice for People in Prison, by Barb Toews

The Little Book of Cool Tools for Hot Topics, by Ron Kraybill and Evelyn Wright

El Pequeño Libro de Justicia Restaurativa, by Howard Zehr

The Little Book of Dialogue for Difficult Subjects, by Lisa Schirch and David Campt

The Little Book of Victim Offender Conferencing, by Lorraine Stutzman Amstutz

The Little Book of Restorative Justice for Colleges and Universities, by David R. Karp

The Little Book of Restorative Justice for Sexual Abuse, by Judah Oudshoorn
with Michelle Jackett and Lorraine Stutzman Amstutz

*The Big Book of Restorative Justice: Four Classic Justice & Peacebuilding Books in One
Volume,* by Howard Zehr, Lorraine Stutzman Amstutz, Allan MacRae, and Kay Pranis

The Little Book of Transformative Community Conferencing, by David Anderson Hooker

The Little Book of Restorative Justice in Education, by Katherine Evans
and Dorothy Vaandering

The Little Book of Restorative Justice for Older Adults, by Julie Friesen and Wendy Meek

The Little Book of Race and Restorative Justice, by Fania E. Davis

The Little Book of Racial Healing, by Thomas Norman DeWolf, Jodie Geddes

The Little Book of Restorative Teaching Tools,
by Lindsey Pointer, Kathleen McGoey, and Haley Farrar

The Little Book of Police Youth Dialogue, by Dr. Micah E. Johnson and Jeffrey Weisberg

The Little Book of Youth Engagement in Restorative Justice, by Evelín Aquino,
Heather Bligh Manchester, and Anita Wadhwa

The Little Book of Restorative Justice Program Design, by Alisa Del Tufo and E. Quin Gonell

Little Book of Listening by Sharon Browning, Donna Duffey, Fred Magondu,
John A. Moore, and Patricia A. Way

Little Book of Restorative Justice for Campus Sexual Harms
by Rachel Roth Sawatzky and Mikayla W-C McCray

The Little Books of Justice & Peacebuilding present, in highly accessible form, key concepts
and practices from the fields of restorative justice, conflict transformation, and peacebuilding.
Written by leaders in these fields, they are designed for practitioners, students, and anyone
interested in justice, peace, and conflict resolution.

The Little Books of Justice & Peacebuilding series is a cooperative effort between the Center
for Justice and Peacebuilding of Eastern Mennonite University and publisher Good Books.

LITTLE BOOK OF

Restorative Teaching Tools

FOR ONLINE LEARNING

*Games and Activities for Restorative
Justice Practitioners*

KATHLEEN McGOEY
AND LINDSEY POINTER

Good Books

New York, New York

Good Books books may be purchased in bulk at special discounts for sales promotion, corporate gifts, fund-raising, or educational purposes. Special editions can also be created to specifications. For details, contact the Special Sales Department, Good Books, 307 West 36th Street, 11th Floor, New York, NY 10018 or info@skyhorsepublishing.com.

Good Books is an imprint of Skyhorse Publishing, Inc.®, a Delaware corporation.

Visit our website at www.goodbooks.com.

10 9 8 7 6 5 4 3 2 1

Library of Congress Cataloging-in-Publication Data is available on file.

Cover design by Kai Texel
Cover photo by Howard Zehr
Illustrations by Colleen McGuire
Series editor: Barb Toews

Print ISBN: 978-1-68099-921-1
Ebook ISBN: 978-1-68099-938-9

Printed in the United States of America

Contents

Chapter 1
Introduction

Not long ago, we, along with many fellow restorative justice educators, doubted that online spaces could match the feeling and experience of in-person teaching and training. We were skeptical that gathering virtually could generate the immersive and connected learning environment needed to teach restorative justice well.

How could people experience deep empathy and connection while looking at faces in little squares on a flat screen?

How could people feel motivated to participate and engage with others in an online class while overcoming distractions or isolation they might be experiencing at home?

How could the "magic" of restorative circles be experienced without sitting side-by-side in a circle?

In March 2020, we were preparing to celebrate the publication of *The Little Book of Restorative Teaching Tools* when the pandemic began and everything shut down. Up until that point, all of the games and activities we had developed were intended for teaching in person. As social distancing guidelines were put in place, we found ourselves adapting quickly and working to figure out how to facilitate many of our favorite games and activities over virtual meeting platforms.

Soon, we weren't just adapting existing games and activities for online use, we were also designing brand-new activities that embraced the strengths of online engagement and used tools such as the chat feature and breakout rooms to make virtual learning more participatory, collective, and fun. We prioritized our commitment to restorative pedagogy (outlined in *The Little Book of Restorative Teaching Tools*) in our facilitation of virtual learning spaces. The result was a collection of games and activities specific to teaching restorative justice online that we are excited to share with you in this book.

This book was also shaped by the learning needs we received from restorative justice practitioners and requests for activities to help teach specific concepts and skills. We are grateful to everyone who reached out to us with requests and ideas. One thing we heard was a need for more ways to spark dialogue and build understanding about structural sources of harm and racism in restorative justice work. As the Black Lives Matter movement increased awareness of racism across contexts, BIPOC restorative justice practitioners and advocates continued to speak and write about the prevalence of racism in restorative justice implementation. Books like *Colorizing Restorative Justice* and *The Little Book of Race and Restorative Justice* provided important, nuanced insight on this topic. Over the past three years, we continued our own learning and critical reflection on our privilege and responsibility as white-bodied, cis-gendered restorative justice practitioners. We worked to develop more activities

2

to help learners understand and address racism and structural injustices as related to restorative justice. These new activities are included in this book.

This book is designed as a sequel to *The Little Book of Restorative Teaching Tools*. We will not be reviewing the material on restorative pedagogy, experiential learning, building restorative learning communities, the inner work required in preparing to teach, or designing an activity-based class or training. However, all of that material is relevant and crucial in preparing to facilitate the games and activities in this book. We recommend you take time to engage with Chapters 1 through 7 of *The Little Book of Restorative Teaching Tools* before diving in here.

The games and activities in this book are intended to support *synchronous* online teaching and training, with the participants and teacher or facilitator meeting live in a virtual space. Some of the games and activities included may be adapted for *asynchronous* or pre-recorded online teaching and training, but the intended mode of delivery is through a live video meeting platform.

Restorative justice is a paradigm shift and collection of practices that has ignited the passionate commitment of many practitioners, advocates, and scholars around the world. As awareness of restorative justice spreads, more and more people are motivated to learn about the field and its guiding concepts and values. Depending on where someone lives, they may have easy access to restorative justice programs or educational opportunities in their geographic region, or they may find there are very few opportunities for restorative justice learning available nearby. The need for people all over the world to be able to access restorative justice education and training is fueling the proliferation of online offerings that have made learning about restorative justice significantly more accessible and affordable. The coronavirus pandemic accelerated this expansion of online learning opportunities and pushed the field to apply greater attention and creativity in how to facilitate, teach, and train online. We hope this book will be a useful contribution to this important growth in online resources that increase access to restorative justice education worldwide.

Chapter 2
Teaching Online

Prior to 2020, the majority of restorative justice teaching, training, and facilitation was done in person, making it difficult to imagine how the same work could be successfully facilitated online. For many restorative justice practitioners, the dramatic shift to connecting virtually was met with resistance and skepticism. Utilizing online platforms for practices that center relationships seemed like a giant hurdle.

Since 2020, virtual classes and training have become a new norm. While the shift to virtual platforms was not easy, it offered opportunities for restorative justice practitioners to be creative in overcoming limitations of screen-based gathering. This chapter outlines some of the most significant challenges of teaching online that impact facilitators' ability to create a restorative learning environment. It provides guidance for facilitators to predict and plan for these challenges, and suggestions for how to bring restorative values to life when engaging learners in a virtual setting.

Cultivating Connection

Perhaps one of the greatest difficulties of teaching virtually is the absence of the informal connection time that often happens in the periods just before, after, or during breaks in an in-person training or class. In a virtual setting, participants don't have the opportunity to mingle and connect with each other during downtime, and are limited in how they can communicate with the facilitator as well. This often means people are entering into the learning process without much sense of who is there with them, and, perhaps more importantly, how others are feeling as they arrive. Without being able to greet and observe learners as they would in a physical space, facilitators lose valuable moments of social intuition to sense what learners might need as they begin the class.

This deficit of informal socializing elevates the need to prioritize time for relationship building and connection at the beginning and throughout an online training or class session. The Activities to Build Relationships in Chapter 4 are specifically designed to build connection and invite all participants to share something personal. A simple opportunity to share can go a long way in setting the stage for a restorative learning experience. Interpersonal connection can open a path for cultivating compassion and curiosity. And as a facilitator, you can observe how participants are showing up from the very start, and make adjustments as needed to create an interactive, inclusive atmosphere.

In addition to activities designed to build relationships, starting with a circle process is one effective method for initiating connection and creating awareness about who is present, as well as their mood or emotional state. You will need to establish a circle order to help participants know who to pass to (since they will not be sitting together in a physical circle).

Here are a couple ways to establish a circle order:

- Post a list of the names of participants in the chat to indicate the order in which people will speak.
- Ask participants to pick someone to pass to after they share until everyone has had an opportunity to share. This works best in smaller groups that are familiar with each other and isn't recommended in larger groups when it is difficult to keep track of who has shared, or in groups with less familiarity where it may add stress for participants.

With both methods, instruct participants to pass to the next person in the circle order verbally by saying, for example, "I pass to you, Kathleen." You may add to this passing ritual by inviting people to bring their own talking piece to hold while they share and pretend to pass through the camera to the next person. When using this method, asking people to share their talking piece and why they chose it presents a good relationship-building opportunity. You can also invite participants to pass with a value or quality of their choice, for example, "I pass to Kathleen with courage" or "I pass to Lindsey with hope."

"One of the things I have found most difficult about teaching online is overcoming the impact of everyone having themselves on mute during video calls. The mute feature is essential because it allows a group to avoid distracting background noises interfering with the ability to hear each other, but it also has the unintended consequence of missing out on the audible laughter and other subtle verbal responses that help us to feel connected to one another. In order to be heard, you have to remember to unmute yourself, and then say what you want to say. This creates a barrier that causes the group to lose some of the spontaneous verbal exchanges that can build relationships, comfort, and group culture so effectively.

"My classes were still fully online when I first facilitated the game 'This or That with a Restorative Twist' (featured in Chapter 4) with a group of students. I asked everyone to unmute themselves for the activity before I gave the instructions and started giving the 'this or that' prompts. As we moved through the first section of low-intensity, relationship-building prompts, it was wonderful to hear the natural laughter from the group and sounds communicating agreement, disbelief, or amusement. It felt like we were in a room together, and trust and connection grew through the next two rounds of prompts about communication styles and bigger 'nature of the universe' questions.

"We finished the activity feeling connected and ready to dive into deeper conversation about the key philosophical issues raised in the third round of prompts. We were able to move seamlessly from the activity into a virtual circle dialogue on the question of forgiveness. 'This or That' provided a way to build the comfort and engagement needed to dive into difficult topics together."

—Lindsey Pointer

Overcoming the Distance

In an in-person class or training, facilitators typically have some degree of control and predictability in the space, allowing them to plan accordingly to set the optimal learning environment for their students. A virtual setting makes it almost impossible to know what kind of room or environment learners are in when they log on to the class. As school teachers experienced during the coronavirus pandemic, some learners will be joining from a noisy, hectic, and distracting space. Others might be completely alone and feel isolated. Others may be fatigued from too much screen time and not enough movement. Facilitators themselves may face difficulty in securing a quiet location with reliable technology that enables them to be fully present to lead an engaging class or training.

Because there is so much the facilitator simply cannot know in advance, the best strategy for overcoming the distance with learners is to provide them information in advance so they know what to expect and can be more present during the class or training itself. You can let them know how to be prepared in writing as well as with verbal reminders. You can send a short video message to learners via email if you think they might not read written instructions. If it is a multi-class series, notify learners at the end of a previous class about what they will need to know for next time. Here are a few important topics to cover in this preparation communication.

1. Privacy and space required

Many activities in this book, as well as others you may utilize for teaching restorative practices, ask participants to speak vulnerably about their own stories, experiences, and growth. Notify participants in advance if they need to find a private space (if possible) so they can feel comfortable sharing openly. Wearing headphones or earbuds helps cancel out background noise.

2. Technology and other setup

Some activities in this book require accessing a document on a shared platform, such as a Google document. Others, such as "What I hear you saying is . . .", ask learners to prepare small slips of paper with a term written on each one. Depending on who your learners are, you can save valuable time and prevent confusion by giving instructions on how to come prepared with setup and any needed materials before the class or training begins.

3. Expectations for participation

It may be helpful for some learners to hear in advance how they are expected to participate. For example, in a participatory learning environment, it is highly rec- ommended that all participants keep their cameras on (to the greatest extent possible). Facilitators may also send other agreements for participation (i.e. norms or ground rules), such as staying muted, how to use the chat, turning off notifications on their devices, and any other specifics to promote respectful, inclusive participation. These agreements should be reviewed again briefly at the beginning of the training.

4. Degree of movement in the space

Inform participants if they will be asked to move around their room/home/office. For example, "Show,

Tell, Ask" invites participants to gather items with personal meaning that they will speak about with others. It may help them to know in advance that they will be asked to move around and gather objects. Always provide adaptations to the activity to allow participation even if a learner is not able to move around their space.

> Be sure to check your assumptions about your participants' access to, and literacy around, technology and online platforms. Participants of all ages and backgrounds may have limited access to devices, stable internet connection, and familiarity with navigating to and around an online platform. It may be necessary to offer short support sessions to brief participants on how to log on to an online session, ensure their camera and microphone are working, and locate different functions. When working in online spaces with local learners, having loaner devices available or providing a physical space from which people can work while participating in an online session will support accessibility and inclusivity.

Attention Fatigue

Learners of all ages will likely demonstrate a shorter attention span online than in person. Become familiar with the online platform you are using and utilize all the functions possible to create variety in the learning experience. Here are a few of the most important and straightforward approaches for holding attention and maintaining engagement.

11

1. Keep instructional segments brief

Depending on the age of your learners, you will want to adjust the duration of time you are speaking and delivering content. Create as much time as possible for questions, dialogue, small group work, and breaks.

2. Incorporate multiple breaks

Invite learners to truly take a break from their screen by standing up and walking away from their device, stepping outside, or getting a glass of water or cup of tea. Consider playing music during breaks to signal the transition time.

3. Encourage learners to move their bodies

Offer prompts for learners to sway, stand up, stretch, and take deep breaths to help them stay present and develop awareness of what their bodies need.

4. Ask learners to answer questions in the chat

This is particularly useful if there isn't enough time for everyone to speak. Read some of the responses out loud to bring attention to learners' shares.

5. Use breakout rooms

Activites in breakout rooms increase connection and opportunity for dialogue. As the facilitator, drop in on breakout rooms to track progress, build relationships, and reinforce learning.

6. Turn on closed captioning and make recordings

These functions improve accessibility for diverse learning needs. Closed captioning will help some learners stay focused. Making recordings available to all participants enables those who miss a session to catch up. For facilitators, watching recordings can assist your self-reflection and debrief after the session.

7. Add variety to your teaching methods
Integrate short video clips, journaling prompts, or opportunities for artistic expression. Diversifying your teaching methods helps hold learners' attention and will improve engagement for people with different learning styles.

"One challenge in teaching, training, and presenting online is groups can be quite large and often the number of participants is less predictable. When teaching or training in person, I like to open with a circle practice to create an opportunity for connection by participants sharing some aspect of their personal story. A circle often isn't possible with large groups online, but there is still a need for connection and interactive ways to build an understanding of restorative justice.

"We developed 'What Did I Need' as a go-to activity for beginning online trainings or presentations with groups of any size. In my experience, this activity actually works better virtually than in person. While participants are free to choose the degree of vulnerability of their shares in any space, people seem to open up more online than they do in person, perhaps due to the distance created by meeting virtually, or possibly due to writing their responses instead of speaking them. And without a great deal of explanation, the activity provides a quick way to get people thinking about how the restorative paradigm feels different by inviting them to reflect on universal human needs and experiences.

"I frequently work with organizations seeking to build restorative workplace culture. When implementing 'What Did I Need' in this context, I simply adjust the questions to ask specifically about experiences of harm in a workplace setting. 'What Did I Need' invites people to reflect and share about their personal experiences without suggesting any one 'right' answer, which parallels storytelling during a restorative justice process. Through their personal reflection, participants gain insight on how restorative justice responds to the needs of every person involved. The activity generates compassion and a sense of connection as participants read one another's responses and find commonalities."

—Kathleen McGoey

Facilitator Affect and Support

When teaching or training virtually, facilitators miss out on the opportunity to set the tone in the space through their own posture and movement, which can establish kinesthetic connection and resonance nonverbally. Instead, they can use their affect and energy level to build the atmosphere of the online learning space. It is important to take time to center yourself before initiating an online session, and consider what kind of affect you want to bring to the space to support your learning objectives. For example, the activity "This or That with a Restorative Twist" requires high energy and enthusiasm, with a playful and upbeat attitude. On the other hand, "Finding Inspiration from Nature" will benefit from a facilitator using a calm, even tone that cues learners to find a sense of peace and spaciousness. We discuss the importance of centering yourself and being mindful of how you are showing up as a facilitator in "Preparing to Teach" in *The Little Book of Restorative Teaching Tools*. This process will look different for every facilitator, and may include going for a walk, sitting quietly, having a snack, or simple breathwork.

When teaching online, you can expect some technological difficulties will impact you or someone else in the session. Reduce the consequences of these difficulties by working with a co-facilitator or tech assistant whenever possible. This person can provide a great deal of help around issues that are difficult to solve in the moment when you are managing a group virtually. A second facilitator (or tech support) acts as a copilot and can manage various tasks such as creating breakout rooms, presenting a screenshare, or taking turns with teaching and facilitation. They can also help learners behind the scenes as individual problems arise. Working as a facilitation team is generally advised in restorative spaces, and in a virtual setting, a co-facilitator can help share the responsibility of tracking the experience of individual participants, maintaining engagement, and providing additional perspective through reflection and debrief.

Teaching, training, and facilitating online carries its own set of challenges and opportunities. It is important to be adaptive and creative to make the most of the virtual setting. Through paying attention

15

to cultivating relationships, integrating opportunities for engagment and experiential learning, being mindful of accessibility, and valuing the voice of each participant, a restorative learning environment is achievable online. We encourage you to have fun with it! You may even find that there are wonderful things you can do in an online learning community that wouldn't be possible in person.

Chapter 3
Introduction to the Games and Activities

The following chapters provide in-depth instructions for facilitating games and activities for teaching restorative justice online as well as prompts to support you in debriefing the learning.

The games and activities are organized into four chapters:

- Chapter 4—Games and activities for building relationships and encouraging meaningful connection and personal sharing among your community of learners.
- Chapter 5—Games and activities to help learners understand and internalize the restorative justice philosophy and the paradigm shift at the root of restorative work.
- Chapter 6—Games and activities to support the development and practice of relevant skills such as identifying feelings and needs at the root of behavior, reflective statements, and reframing.

- Chapter 7—Games and activities to support learners in understanding and addressing structural and racial injustices.

Instructions and links to materials (when applicable), along with additional games and activities, are available at restorativeteachingtools.com.

The activities included in this book make use of video call technology (such as Zoom) and many require the screenshare, chat, or breakout room features. Please take time to familiarize yourself with those features in advance of teaching or facilitating. When groups are working in breakout rooms, it can be helpful to send messages through the broadcast function to let them know how much time they have left around the ten, five, or three-minute marks. Consider visiting each breakout room at some point during the work time to support discussions. The activities were not designed for hybrid environments (where some people are online and some are in person). If you would like to use the activities in a hybrid setting, we recommend careful planning and practicing so you can troubleshoot challenges in advance.

As you prepare to use the games and activities in the following chapters, we encourage you to engage creatively with the material and think about how to make it most relevant and culturally congruent for your learning community. As authors, we learn something new every time we facilitate, and strive to integrate that learning in the next delivery. This deepens our relationship with the material, improves our facilitation skills, and makes the activities more fun and effective for learners.

Chapter 4
Games and Activities to Build Relationships

Relationship building is fundamental to all restorative justice efforts. Focusing on relationships helps to build the comfort and trust needed for the group to dive into more challenging material, and supports learners' capacity to develop rapport with participants in restorative processes. Gathering online limits some opportunities for connection that occur naturally in a physical space. Because of this, it is particularly important to devote time and effort to building relationships when learning online.

A fast-paced spin on an old game, the first activity in this chapter raises energy, generates laughter, and plants seeds for further dialogue as learners weigh in on their preferences and beliefs, building from lighthearted to more introspective sharing. The second and third activities invite learners to introduce personal objects to the online space as a way to share more about themselves.

"This or That" with a Restorative Twist

Objective
Participants will experience a lively way to connect quickly and learn about others, first by responding to playful and low-risk prompts, followed by prompts that elicit more personal sharing and deeper reflection.

Materials
A written list with three levels of prompts:
- This or That
- Communicate or Bust
- Nature of the Universe

Instructions
Explain that this is an adapted version of the game "This or That." You will be announcing two choices (for example, "burgers or tacos") and every participant has to indicate quickly which one they prefer by using a hand gesture. Demonstrate the two hand gestures, which can be anything you would like. The hand gestures need to have obvious visual differences, and participants must be able to do the hand gesture and still see the screen. For example, raise both hands up with "peace fingers" or hold hands up to both eyes like you are looking through goggles. You will demonstrate each hand gesture and the option it correlates with each time you make the announcement. For example: "Burgers (peace fingers) OR Tacos (goggles)?!" You only need to have two hand gestures which you will use throughout the entire activity.

Start with five to ten simple "This or That" prompts, such as the suggested Level 1 prompts below. If you want to go deeper, progress to Level 2 "Communicate or Bust" prompts, and then to Level 3 "Nature of the Universe" prompts.

This is one of those games where your energy level and approach will set the tone for the game. Announce each set of "This or That" options with some drama or flair, and make sure that you act out the gesture that correlates with each option, every single time. Play along with the group. Keep the game moving and don't dwell on any one prompt for too long, other than to throw in something quick and energizing like, "So many texters! Where are my phone call people?!"

Prompts (use these and/or develop your own!):

Level 1: This or That

Cat	OR	Dog
Ice Cream	OR	Frozen Yogurt
Morning	OR	Night
Save	OR	Spend
Text	OR	Call
Singing	OR	Dancing
Superman	OR	Batman
Sweet	OR	Salty
Money	OR	Fame

Level 2: Communicate or Bust

You're in a conflict:	Runaway and hide	OR	Address it head-on
Apologizing to someone:	Super difficult	OR	Not a problem
You've been confronted:	Yell	OR	Cry
Taking responsibility:	Own up to it proactively	OR	Wait until you've been caught

Level 3: Nature of the Universe

What's more powerful:	Fate	OR	Free will
Trust can be repaired:	For sure	OR	No way
People:	Inherently flawed	OR	Inherently good
True forgiveness happens:	Possible	OR	Impossible
Why we are who we are:	Nature	OR	Nurture
People can change:	Definitely yes	OR	Doubtful

> ## Online Learning Tip
> In any online learning setting, consider how your tone and affect will impact the experience of participants. You may need to slow down and allow for silence to give space for reflection and processing during some activities. Do not be afraid of silence! People need time. On the other hand, you may want to use a light and lively tone to set the mood for activities where you are asking learners to be more creative with storytelling. Demonstrating an affect that aligns with the vibe of the activity itself will give learners cues about how you would like them to engage.

Debrief

The debrief of this game can happen along the way if you notice that some prompts elicit surprising responses and you sense a need for the group to discuss more. Or, you can wait until the end of the game to start the debrief.

- What surprised you about watching the group respond to the prompts?
- What did you learn about this group that you didn't know before?
- What came up that you would like to learn more about?

Lesson

We can get creative about engaging kinesthetically with our learning communities, even if it is via screens. Sometimes connection can happen in short, energetic bursts to break up a long meeting or training just through Level 1 prompts. Or, take the game further for more intentional relationship-building around things like communication styles and beliefs about the nature of the universe. You will likely learn something about yourself or someone else that you didn't know before!

Instructions for In-Person Adaptation

To play this game in person, ask participants to form groups of five or six people and spread the groups out around the room. Each group will stand or sit in a small circle facing one another so they can see which hand gesture each person picks. As the game facilitator, you may need to speak loudly or use a bell to get everyone's attention and give the "This or That" prompts to the full group.

Show, Tell, and Ask

Objective

Participants will build relationships and practice asking open-ended questions.

Materials

For this activity, you will need to establish a circle order. See Chapter 2 for ideas about how to do this.

Instructions

Tell the participants that this activity evokes childhood "Show and Tell" circles and invites them to share personally meaningful objects with the group. Open the activity by sharing the group agreements for the activity. You can use the list below or adapt them for your community:

- Please speak and listen with respect, and share time fairly.
- Respect everyone's privacy. Only tell your own story and do not share what you hear from others outside this circle.
- During this activity, you will be sharing areas or items in your homes. Please be considerate of other people in your home and their needs. If you need to move around your home during this activity and others are present, ask for their consent now to be on camera in shared spaces (pause, if needed).

After reviewing these agreements, ask if there are any additional agreements participants would like to add in order for this to feel like a safe space for

25

sharing. After the list of commitments is complete, ask participants for their agreement. Wait for a nod, thumbs-up, or some other form of agreement from participants.

Ask the "primary" circle question that all participants will respond to. You can select from these options, or create your own based on the comfort level of your group:

- What is an area or object in your home that tells a story about you? Share a few sentences about its significance.
- What is an area or object in your home that brings you comfort? In two or three sentences, tell us why this item or area brings you comfort.
- What is something in your home that helps the group get to know you better? Tell us briefly about what it means to you.

Tell participants that they can either present something by holding it in front of their camera, or, if they're feeling adventurous and have consent to do so, carry their device/camera with them to an area of their home.

The first person in the circle responds to the question by showing the group an area or a thing in their home and explaining its significance. It's just like Show and Tell!

After the first person shows their area or item and describes its significance, the next person in the circle then asks one follow-up question about what the first person shared. Guidelines for these follow-up questions include that the question must:

- Be open-ended
- Have a spirit of enthusiastic curiosity
- Show you sincerely care
- Help us all get to know the person better

The first speaker responds to the follow-up question. After they respond, the person who just asked a follow-up question responds to the primary circle question by showing the group an area or a thing in their home and explaining its significance. The next person in the circle then asks them a follow-up question.

The game continues in this way until everyone has both responded to the primary circle question by showing and telling, and has also asked someone else a follow-up question.

If your group is new to circle practice, or prone to talking over each other in screen-based interactions, you may need to take a more active facilitation role. For example, you may need to direct each turn by saying: "Thank you for sharing. Next, Maya will be doing the Show and Tell, and Casey will ask the follow-up question." At this point in the game, your goal is to add structure. Avoid adding commentary or questions about what participants have shared.

Add another layer of skills-building by having the person asking the follow-up question listen to the first speaker's response, then make a reflective statement before asking a second follow-up question.

Circle participants may need to walk through their home to get to the area or thing they want to show the group. This can be a relational and connective

27

moment as you catch glimpses of pets, family, etc. However, participants can also turn off their video while they move around if that is needed for privacy and safety. Or, they can leave their camera set up in its original place while leaving that room to collect their objects. If you have a sense this activity will make participants uncomfortable sharing their home life, consider telling all participants about the activity in advance and ask them to collect five items to have nearby that they feel comfortable showing and talking about with others.

Debrief
- What is something you heard in someone else's story that you can relate to?
- What inspired or resonated with you?
- How were you impacted by sharing more about your life with others?

Lesson
Making connections with our community is very important, particularly in times of hardship and stress. Each one of us has the ability to be creative in finding ways to connect with others, even from afar.

Instructions for In-Person Adaptation
To use this activity in an in-person learning environment, simply provide participants with the circle prompt ahead of time and ask them to bring the object to the learning space with them. For example, "Please bring an object from home that tells a story about you." All participants will come to the circle

with their objects and the question-asking component of the activity can take place in the same way; participants will just be seated in a physical circle rather than online.

Relational Scavenger Hunt

Objective
Participants will build relationships, get to know each other, and laugh together.

Materials
A list of scavenger hunt prompts.

Instructions
Start by explaining that this is a scavenger hunt in which participants will be asked to move around their homes (or wherever they are) to find objects that relate to a list of prompts. Whoever manages to gather objects to respond to the greatest number of prompts will win (just like a regular scavenger hunt). Participants will have a limited amount of time (two minutes) to collect all objects, so this game is about speed, making quick decisions, and having fun.

Begin with a scavenger hunt warm-up round to get people energized. Announce one item that everyone must find, and give them a very short amount of time to find it. For example:

- **Warm-up 1:** "Find something shiny—you have ten seconds!" Start counting down immediately so people can hear you as they run around to find their shiny item. At the ten-second mark, everyone must be back in front of their screen holding up their shiny item in front of their camera.
- **Warm-up 2:** "Find something smelly—you have seven seconds!"

- **Warm-up 3:** "Find something cuddly—you have eleven seconds!"

Once you have everyone moving and energized, begin the next phase. Post the list of prompts for Round One in the chat. As soon as the prompts have been shared, the timer begins.

Participants have two minutes to run around their space and gather objects that respond to as many of the prompts as possible. You cannot use one object for multiple prompts.

The Round One prompts should create opportunities for group members to get to know each other. For example:

- Find something that always makes you smile when you see it.
- Find something that reminds you of your childhood.
- Find something related to your favorite animal.
- Find something that you have been meaning to get rid of.
- Find a book or magazine that you haven't read yet, but really, really want to read.
- Find a piece of food you are excited to eat today.
- Find something you made.
- Find a gift you were given that meant a lot to you.
- Find an item that makes you feel grateful.
- Find something that reminds you of someone in this group.
- Find an object you would use as a talking piece if you were going to be a circlekeeper with this group.

31

As participants move around their homes gathering objects, loudly announce how much time they have left in a playfully urgent tone. For example, "Hurry up, you have one minute!" "Clock's ticking! Thirty seconds!" and then count down from 10. You may wish to use a buzzer or some other fun sound to indicate when time is up.

When time has run out and everyone is back in front of their cameras, have everyone go around in a circle and share the objects they collected for each prompt, explaining the connection (briefly) as they go. Determine who gathered the most objects and declare a winner for the round.

> Please be mindful of participants' mobility and adapt the game accordingly. For example, you could remove the time pressure element from the instructions, use fewer prompts, and focus the game on connection and storytelling.

In groups that know each other well, play a second round with prompts that reinforce the relationships already built in the group. For example:

- Find something you know will make a specific person in this group laugh.
- Find an item of clothing that you think someone in this group would be likely to wear.
- Find something that represents this group (for example, this family, this community, this class, this circle of friends).

- Find an item that gives you strength during hard times.
- Find something that makes you feel proud to be a member of our community.
- Find something that brings tears to your eyes.
- Find an item you would not share with most people . . . but you are going to let this group in on a secret!
- Find the item that would make the most meaningful or silly centerpiece for a community meal.

If you're confident your group can engage appropriately, consider the following prompts:

- Find something that makes you roll your eyes when you see it.
- Find something that you typically would not want to be visible in the background of your virtual meetings.
- Find something you could wear on your body . . . but you never would!
- Find an item you would love to throw as hard as you possibly could against a concrete wall.

Debrief
- What is one new or interesting thing you learned about someone else?
- What is a connection you found with another person?

Lesson

Restorative practices are all about relationships. This is an opportunity to build relationships in a fun and active way that breaks up the sedentary nature of online classes or trainings.

Online Learning Tip

As facilitator, it is important that you participate as well! As discussed in *The Little Book of Restorative Teaching Tools,* applying a restorative pedagogical approach means that facilitators and teachers are also participating in the learning process. Your participation in this and other activities helps shift the power differential that exists between teacher and students in conventional education models. It also supports you in developing closer, more authentic relationships with participants and building community.

Chapter 5
Games and Activities to Understand the Restorative Philosophy

A restorative pedagogical approach asks learners to interact intrapersonally and interpersonally with restorative principles and values. It urges us to expand our thinking to imagine when and how these values may be applied in our own lives, past and present. These activities invite learners to step into restorative frameworks and try them on through reflection, application to lived experience, and creative expression. Through this process, learners will develop clarity and confidence as practitioners who seek to integrate a more restorative orientation and approach in their lives.

What Did I Need?

Objective

Participants reflect on the needs they experienced from three perspectives: after hearing about a crime in their community, after being harmed by another person, and after causing harm to another person. This self-reflection about personal experiences provides a springboard for understanding what makes the restorative approach to justice distinct and powerful.

Material

No materials required.

Instructions

This activity works well at the beginning of an online presentation or workshop to provide an introduction to restorative justice. It can be used with a group of any size.

Explain to participants that they will be using the chat function to respond to a series of questions. You will pose the questions verbally, but for visual learners, you may want to have the questions written on slides that you share, or you can copy and paste each question into the chat one-by-one.

Explain that you are going to start with a few relationship-building questions to help the group get to know each other. This serves a dual purpose of generating a sense of connection in the group (like opening with a circle) while also building participants' comfort using the chat function to respond to questions. If you dive right into the deeper, more difficult questions, you will likely have fewer people engage. It is important to use a scaffolded approach by starting with a few simple relationship-building questions.

Here are some examples of relationship-building questions you may want to ask in the chat. Feel free to be as creative as you wish!

- How many siblings do you have? (Include half-siblings, adopted, or step-siblings)
- What is the most interesting form of transportation you have used?
- What is the most unusual job you have had?
- If you could have one thing floating next to you in the air at all times, so that you could access it any time you wanted, what would it be?

Ask each question one at a time and read out loud some of the responses as they appear in the chat. You may also share your own response to each question.

Thank everyone for taking the time to answer the relationship-building questions and explain that the questions will now shift to be related to the topic of restorative justice. There will be three prompts and a closing from the facilitator.

Prompt 1
Reflect on a time that, as a member of your community, you became aware that a crime had been committed. You were not directly involved. What were your needs as a community member? Write some of the needs you experienced in the chat.

As responses appear in the chat, read some out loud and note points of overlap. You may also want to share some of the needs you've experienced as a community member. For example, "I needed information. I wanted to know what happened and what was being done about it, so I could feel safe."

Prompt 2

Think back to a time that you experienced harm directly. Maybe you were the victim of a crime or maybe it was an instance in your personal life when you were wronged by another person. What were your needs? Please write them in the chat box.

As responses appear in the chat, read some out loud and note points of commonality. You may also want to share some needs you have experienced when you were harmed. For example, "I needed the person who harmed me to know how it had impacted my life. I needed to know they wouldn't do it again to me or anyone else. I wanted to know that they understood what they had done and that they were sorry." Or "I needed someone to fix the damage to my property." Or, "I needed validation of how painful it was." Or "I needed to get my questions answered."

Online Learning Tip

Whenever you ask participants to add their thoughts to the chat, take time to read through what they've written. As you read, speak some of the written shares out loud. Add a reflection when you read something that you'd like to validate or highlight. Ask a clarifying question when you read something that intrigues you or you think could create more learning for all.

Prompt 3:

Finally, think back on a time when you caused harm to another person. Maybe you committed a crime or hurt someone, intentionally or not, through your words or actions. Following the incident when your actions caused harm, what were your needs?

As responses appear in the chat, read some out loud and note any trends. You may also want to share some needs you have experienced as someone who has caused harm. For example, "I needed to take responsibility and be able to apologize and do something to try to make it right. I also wanted others to know that it was a mistake and I felt regret." Or "I needed to share with the person I hurt about what was going through my mind at that time. I wanted to be understood."

Thank everyone for sharing. Explain that it is helpful to start a conversation on restorative justice by reflecting on the needs that emerge following crime, wrongdoing, or incidents of harm because the goal of addressing needs is central in restorative approaches.

Debrief

You may choose to ask participants to respond to debrief questions in the chat or you can ask for a few volunteers to speak up to share their reflections from the activity. Asking participants to unmute and speak at this time creates a nice change of pace.

- What insight did you gain from reflecting on the needs you experienced in various roles following incidents of harm?

39

- What trends or commonalities did you notice as everyone responded from the three different perspectives?
- How did this exercise impact your understanding of restorative justice?

Lesson

One of the defining features of restorative justice is how it creates a space to understand and respond to the needs of all individuals following incidents of harm, including the harmed person, responsible person, and broader community.

> Taking time to reflect on our own experiences helps to cultivate empathy for the participants in restorative processes and to understand the central importance of identifying, validating, and responding to individual and collective needs.

Five Rs Stories

Objective

Participants will learn about the restorative approach to crime and conflict by engaging with the five Rs of restorative justice, a framework outlined by Beverly Title in *Teaching Peace: A Restorative Justice Framework for Strengthening Relationships* (Del Hayes Press, 2011).

Materials

- Decks of ten cards that include five cards with the five restorative justice "R" words on them, one "R" word per card (Relationship, Respect, Responsibility, Repair, and Reintegration) and five cards with five punitive "R" words on them, one "R" word per card (Revenge, Retaliation, Ranting, Rage, and Recklessness).
- A story prompt.

Note: For this activity, participants will be in small groups and each group will make their own deck of cards. It is helpful to have a sample deck to show participants what they will create.

Instructions

This activity involves collaborative storytelling. It invites creative silliness in exploring punitive plot twists in storytelling for the sake of contrast. Before playing, please consider whether or not your learners will be able to engage in a way that is playfully appropriate without getting outrageous or being offensive to others.

41

Start by establishing groups of two to five people that you will send into breakout rooms after giving instructions. Each group will be a storytelling team.

Before sending them into the breakout rooms, ask one person from each group to be the card dealer for their team. This person will make the deck of ten "R" words—five restorative justice "R" words and five punitive "R" words—and shuffle the deck so all the "R" words are mixed randomly into one deck. It is helpful to show them an example of the ten cards.

Provide the storytelling teams with a prompt to start the story (see examples below). The prompt should include a crime or conflict, but to maintain the silly and lighthearted nature of this game, select a crime or conflict scenario that isn't too egregious. Share the written scenario with the large group via the chat while giving instructions, and they will still be able to see it in their breakout rooms. Instruct learners to unmute themselves for the entirety of the storytelling process in their breakout rooms.

Sample Stories

1. Evan and Holly live in a townhouse in a large city in a row of identical homes. Holly purchases a large potted plant at a fundraiser for her niece's school, which they place outside their front door. Holly is very fond of the plant. One day, they wake up and see that the plant is missing. They are upset and confused. Two days later, on a walk in their neighborhood, they notice the same plant is sitting outside the front door of a neighbor's house a few blocks down the street from them. They know it is the same plant because it has Holly's niece's initials carved into the pot.

2. Marcus, age sixteen, is about to leave for a four-week summer school trip to Guatemala. He is excited, nervous, and very worried about what is going to happen with his new relationship with his girlfriend Ria while he's away. The night before his international flight, Marcus decides to sneak out to spend a little more time with Ria before he leaves. Marcus climbs out a small window in the basement of his house. He leaves a candle burning on the windowsill so he'll be able to find his way back inside more easily in the dark. When Marcus returns home at 4:30 a.m., the candle is out and there is a note waiting for him in his dad's handwriting: "We need to talk on our way to the airport. See you at 6 a.m."

The card dealer for each team will start with the cards in a pile, face down. They will read the story prompt and then draw a card from the pile. The card will have one of the five restorative "R" words or one of the five punitive "R" words written on it. They will hold the card up to their camera so the others can see the word they drew.

The card dealer will then use that "R" word as a guiding theme to describe what happens next in the story. They will share several sentences with the group following that theme. After building the story with a few lines, they will pause and pass to the next person. When they pass, the card dealer will pull the next card and hold it up to their camera so that everyone in the storytelling team can see. Person 2 continues the story influenced by the "R" word that was drawn for them. After a few lines, they will pause and pass to the next person. Again, the card dealer will pull a card, hold it up to their camera, and Person 3 will pick up the storyline in the direction of that "R" word. The game continues with each storytelling team member having a card drawn for them and adding to the story until either 1) all "R" words have been drawn or 2) all team members have had a turn.

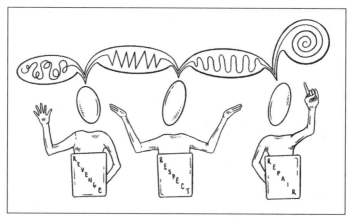

Example

Person 1 (the card dealer) reads the story prompt:

"Evan and Holly live in a townhouse in a large city in a row of identical homes. Holly purchases a large potted plant at a fundraiser for her niece's school, which they place outside their front door. She is very fond of the plant. One day, they wake up and see that the plant is missing. They are upset and confused. Two days later, on a walk in their neighborhood, they notice the same plant is sitting outside the front door of a neighbor's house a few blocks down the street from them. They know it is the same plant because it has Holly's niece's initials carved into the pot."

Person 1 (the card dealer) draws the "Respect" card and adds to the story:

"Evan and Holly decide the best thing to do is to knock on the door and politely ask the person who answers why they have the potted plant and explain that it is theirs. They knock on the door."

Person 2 draws the "Rage" card and adds to the story:

"When a man answers the door, they are suddenly overcome by rage. 'What is wrong with you?' Holly screams. 'We are taking this back!' she asserts as she delivers a swift kick to a gnome statue the neighbor had placed by the potted plant."

Person 3 draws the "Revenge" card and adds to the story:

"That night, Evan and Holly sneak back to the neighbor's and egg his house."

Person 4 draws the "Repair" card and adds to the story:

"When they wake up in the morning, they feel bad about what they did and go back to the neighbor's house to apologize. They explain how meaningful the potted plant was to them and the impact of having it suddenly disappear. They listen to the impacts the neighbor experienced when they screamed and kicked his favorite garden gnome. They offer to replace the gnome and clean up the mess."

Person 5 draws the "Reintegration" card and adds to the story:

"Evan and Holly decide to host a neighborhood barbecue in their front yard and invite the neighbor who had taken the potted plant to bring his famous potato salad."

After the collaborative storytelling process is complete using the restorative and punitive "R" words, bring everyone back from breakout rooms. Ask for a few reflections from the group and then instruct the storytelling teams to take just the five restorative "R" words (Relationship, Respect, Responsibility, Repair, and Reintegration) and put them in a pile in that order with "Relationship" on the top.

Send the groups back to their breakout rooms and ask them to go through the collaborative storytelling process again, but this time with only the five restorative "R" words and in this specific order: Relationship, Respect, Responsibility, Repair, and Reintegration. Notice how the five Rs build on each other to create a restorative process and outcome in the wake of crime and conflict.

This step of repeating the collaborative storytelling process again with only the five restorative "R" words is essential for landing the lesson of this activity and showing how a restorative approach to crime or conflict can result in a transformative outcome for all involved.

Debrief

- How did introducing the restorative values through the five Rs influence the progression of the story?
- How is this activity of intentionally applying the five Rs relevant to your life, or your work as a practitioner?

Lesson

Restorative justice is flexible across environments and scenarios, but the guiding principles and values help us orient to a restorative mindset and approach. It is helpful to recognize and accept that we live in societies and cultures that are conditioned by punitive, adversarial frameworks. Choosing a restorative approach requires intention.

Instructions for In-Person Adaptation

When playing this game in person, give each group a physical deck of the cards. Group members sit in a circle and pass the deck around the circle so that each person is drawing their own "R" word from the deck and then continuing the story according to the "R" word they draw from the deck.

"What is RJ?" in Three Minutes

Objective

They say that the best way to learn something is to teach others. This activity gives those learning about restorative justice an opportunity to more deeply integrate the restorative philosophy and approach by creatively explaining it to others in a concise way.

Material

A phone, computer, or camera for participants to record a video.

Instructions

Provide the following description and instructions. Be sure to give learners plenty of time (at least a week) to complete this project so that they have time to brainstorm and experiment, and tell them the due date in your instructions.

> *"What is restorative justice?" That is an important question that can be difficult to answer! Being able to describe restorative justice in a concise way is a useful skill. This activity gives you a chance to prac-tice that skill and engage your creativity.*
>
> *Record a three-minute video that answers the question "What is restorative justice?" Feel free to take a creative approach by integrating art, poetry, symbolism, metaphors, or anything that sparks your imagination that you think would help create a broader understanding of restorative justice philos-ophy and practice. The sky is the limit! We will be watching the videos together as a group and will use*

a circle process to debrief the experience of creating them and give each other feedback.

"I love doing this activity with groups and am always amazed by the creative approaches students take. One favorite was a video that showed hands quilting while a voice described restorative justice through the metaphor of a quilt. Another memorable video involved a student reciting a moving poem she wrote about an incident of harm within her family and how she now sees it through a restorative lens."

—Lindsey Pointer

Debrief

After watching the videos together as a group (using the screenshare function) and appreciating everyone's work, use a circle process to debrief the experience and give each other feedback. Possible debrief circle questions include:

- What is something in another person's video that really resonated or felt particularly effective in communicating restorative justice?
- What surprised you about the similarities or differences in the approach and content of the videos?
- What have you learned about how to communicate about restorative justice effectively?

Lesson

Being able to communicate restorative justice philosophy with others is an important skill and an opportunity to be creative. Describing restorative justice through your own personal lens and experience can often provide the clearest and most meaningful description for others who are new to the subject.

Social Relational Window Shuffle

Objective
Students will internalize the restorative approach to conflict, behavior, and harm. They will understand and be able to contrast the restorative approach with other approaches (neglectful, permissive, and punitive).

Materials
- A Social Relational Window visual on your computer that you can show through screenshare.
- Conflict scenarios that are relevant to your group and their context (for example, if you are working with school staff, use school-based scenarios that relate to their work and daily interactions).

Note: You need four or more participants to play this game.

Instructions
Begin by offering a basic introduction to the Social Relational Window model. The Social Relational Window is based on both Paul McCold's and Ted Wachtel's "Social Discipline Window" and Dorothy Vaandering's "Relationship Widow."* The Social Relational

---

* For more information about Paul McCold and Ted Wachtel's "Social Discipline Window" and Dorothy Vaandering's "Relationship Window" and the decisions we made to adapt the model for this activity, see https://restorativeteachingtools.com/understanding-the-social-relational-window/.

Window describes four basic approaches to maintaining social norms and behavioral boundaries. The four approaches are represented as different combinations of high or low expectations of behaviors and high or low support. High expectations of behavior paired with low support is a punitive or "to" approach. High support paired with low expectations of behavior is a permissive or "for" approach. Low support paired with low expectations of behavior is a neglectful or "not" approach. The restorative domain combines high expectations of behavior with high support and is characterized by doing things "with" people, rather than "to" them or "for" them. As you are explaining this conceptual tool, it is helpful to use one simple, relatable scenario from your life to give a brief example of each response. For example, we often use the example of someone we live with not washing their dishes, and describe briefly what neglectful, permissive, punitive, and restorative responses to that scenario look like as we describe the model. For example,

To: You tell your roommate they have to wash their dishes within thirty minutes of every meal or snack. If they don't comply, you will start storing clean dishes in your bedroom so your roommate can't use them.

For: You start waking up earlier than usual to be sure you have time to walk around the house, collect all the dirty dishes, and wash them before you start using the kitchen. You load the dishwasher in the morning, then unload the dishwasher in the evening. You do this quietly and don't mention the inconvenience to your roommate.

Not: You simply ignore the dirty dishes and do not address the person who hasn't been washing them.

You don't touch the dirty dishes, and don't say anything to anyone about the situation and how you feel.

With: You ask your roommate for a conversation and explain how you are affected by the dirty dishes in the house. You dialogue about each of your needs and expectations around the dishes and house cleanliness in general. You co-create agreements that will meet each person's needs.

Read a conflict scenario to the whole group and explain that they will be coming up with the "not," "to," "for," and "with" responses to the scenario. Next, divide the group into four teams. Tell the teams they will have three minutes to work together before coming back to the large group and then send them into their breakout rooms. Join each of the breakout rooms one by one to assign each team the quadrant of the Social Relational Window they are responsible for ("not," "to," "for," or "with"). Leave the teams in their breakout rooms and give them about five minutes to work together to formulate a response to the conflict that matches their quadrant (for example, the "for" team has to come up with a permissive response to the scenario).

Online Learning Tip

Whenever you drop in on breakout rooms, expect to encounter questions and needs for clarification from learners. In this activity and others, you will need to move quickly from one room to the next. Prepare in advance and communicate with your co-facilitator during preparation about how you will do this efficiently.

When time is up, end the breakout rooms and bring everyone back together. Each team takes a turn to either act out or describe their response to the scenario (this activity becomes much more engaging and lively if teams act out their response instead of explaining it). Ask the other teams to identify which quadrant the presented response fits in and why. Allow the presenting team to announce which quadrant was theirs. Discuss each response type:

- What is the impact of each response?
- What works or does not work about the "to" response? The "for" response? The "not" response?
- What is effective about the "with" response? How could it be made even more restorative?

Repeat the process with one or two additional scenarios, assigning "to," "for," "not," and "with" to different teams so that each team has a chance to practice and internalize multiple approaches and what makes them different.

Debrief
- What are the benefits of the "with" approach? As you go about your life, how can you remember to approach issues restoratively?
- Reflecting on the different areas of your life (work, family, friends, etc.), what is your default response to harm and conflict? How can you use this tool as a mental map to orient toward a restorative response?

- When have you experienced each of these responses in your life, and how did each one impact your relationships?

Lesson
You can choose to use restorative approaches in all areas of your life. What differentiates a restorative approach from other approaches is maintaining a dynamic balance between offering support and holding high expectations for behavior. Accountability and understanding are equally important. Achieving this balance takes practice and requires mindfulness and compassion.

Instructions for In-Person Adaptation
Instructions for playing this game in person can be found in *The Little Book of Restorative Teaching Tools.*

Inspiration from Nature to Deepen Our Practice

Objective

Relax and observe. The natural world offers many lessons to help us ground, trust, and deepen our understanding of so much: change, systems, interdependence. Allowing ourselves to slow down and pause simply to notice provides an opportunity to amplify our perception with all senses. Reflecting on and integrating our perceptions of nature engages imagination and stimulates creativity. This activity is an invitation for you to pause, observe, wonder, and reflect as an individual, or in a group of learners. Our hope is the process will deepen the creative capacity you bring to restorative practices while also offering you a holistic restorative respite wherever you are. This activity is also an invitation to step away from screens and spend time outside.

Materials

This activity can be done individually or in a group. Anyone participating needs materials they enjoy using for reflection and expression, such as a journal, art supplies, a musical instrument, or props for physical movement. If doing this activity as a group, ask participants to prepare by gathering the materials they would like to use.

We highly recommend reading *Emergent Strategy: Shaping Change, Changing Worlds* by adrienne maree brown (AK Press, 2017) to support this activity. brown shares observations of starlings, mycelium, water, and more as examples of the many ways social movements and activists can learn from the natural world. These observations were a central inspiration for this activity. In her book, brown provides reference to artists, authors, thinkers, and groups who offer insight about these concepts and will help prompt your imagination!

> "I have become obsessed with how we can be movements like flocks of birds, underground power like whispering mushrooms, the seashell representation of a galactic vision for justice— small patterns that avoid useless predation, spread lessons, and proliferate change.
>
> Emergent strategies let us practice, in every possible way, the world we want to see."
> —adrienne maree brown, *Emergent Strategy: Shaping Change, Changing Worlds*

Instructions

If you are doing this activity with a group, gather online first to give the instructions below. You may want to screenshare these instructions and ask a participant to read them out loud. Make sure everyone understands what to do. You will then end the online meeting to give everyone approximately one hour of time on their own. This exercise can also be assigned as homework, or offered as something to be completed during participants' free time. Be clear that this activity requires everyone to step away from all screens and devices. It may help participants to power down their devices or put them on airplane mode. If you plan to gather to debrief, set a time for everyone to reconvene on the online platform. A sample introduction is as follows.

For this activity, we invite you to set aside one hour of uninterrupted time in a place you feel safe. The first step is to slow down, become quiet, and get outdoors if possible. If you cannot be outdoors, reach into your memories or imagination to explore the natural world. With either approach, you may need to walk, meditate, or use other mindfulness practices to become present. First, notice. Notice objects or symbols that attract your attention, and follow those. Sit with a tree, gaze at a flower, stare at the sky, rub a blade of grass. Or in your mind, let your vision drift upward as you watch a tree branch swaying, or gaze at water flowing around smooth river rocks. What do you hear? Smell? Taste? See? Feel? Take time to become fully aware of each of your senses. Pause and notice. If your mind wanders, kindly and gently bring it back. Stay present in this space for at least thirty minutes.

Second, reflect and express. Pick up your journal, art supplies, musical instrument, or anything that stimulates your creativity. Draw, write, or create anything that comes to mind related to your noticing. Anything goes! It is helpful to be in a "yes, and" space; avoid judging or filtering whatever comes up. Widen your perspective to consider metaphors and symbols. Keep going until you feel complete.

Debrief

This is an activity that does not require a debrief. One's own experience in the activity holds meaning and value just as it is. If you and your community would like to debrief, consider doing so with a circle process in your online gathering space. Through rounds of sharing in circle, invite participants to share both verbally and nonverbally. While validation and discussion can help to deepen the reflective process, avoid evaluating or comparing experiences. Respect the value of each person's unique experience by guiding the group not to assess or assign meaning to others' shares.

Lesson

Cultivating creativity helps restorative skills thrive. Practicing being present and listening with all senses supports our well-being and our work as restorative practitioners. The natural world is full of incredible models and motivation for the restorative social movement!

An Example from Kathleen

On a recent family vacation to the beach, I was captivated by crabs. First, it was crabs on a cement step that bordered the ocean, where I watched crabs getting drenched by sporadic ocean waves that appeared to pound their tiny shells, drain and recede, then wash over them again. The crabs seemed content to remain still while the waves came again and again, then suddenly, during a break in the waves, they'd bolt across the step, presumably to snatch up some tasty micro-organic treat. Stillness . . . then a quick burst of movement. They looked un-fazed (or perhaps acutely aware) by the chaos of the waves, their timing, their pre-dicted force and impact.

Later, sitting very still in the sand, I watched as crabs that had been completely invisible, hid-ing just under the surface of the sand, revealed themselves. When there were no humans or other sources of movement nearby, one crab popped up and skittered quickly across the sand. Then another, and another. I wondered how much they were sensing one another as much as the absence of threat. I watched and wondered, and looked for the crabs throughout my vacation. I recognized my complete lack of knowledge of crab facts, and instead, inspired by *Emergent Strategy*, delighted in wondering about them and what I might learn through observation and imagination.

I reflected on how, for a couple years, I've tried to confront and transform beliefs I've ascribed to for so long about time and urgency. Beliefs I have come to understand originate in dominant culture and conditioning. These beliefs are guided by scarcity thinking, and direct me and others to keep moving: keep moving to improve, to make a difference, to make change in your cause or mission. Don't waste time, be productive. Do more. Don't stop. One more thing. Running out of time . . . never enough!

But what about the lessons of the crabs? What about staying still, waiting, listening, watching, until the time is right to move? What about pausing and trusting? What about valuing stillness as much (or more) as action? What about knowing the waves (potential threats) so well that you can let them splash, slam, create chaos all around, and remain still, just present and trusting that the time to move will become clear. Remaining focused, attentive, training the senses to relax and attune, to find gentle awareness in place of constant vigilance.

A year and a half after reflecting on my experience with the crabs, Lindsey sent me a podcast about the secret intelligence and life of crabs. I was delighted to learn about crabs' "real life" capacities and highly adaptable nature. My learning was enriched by the time I had spent observing the crabs and the world I had imagined simply by watching and wondering.

Chapter 6
Games and Activities for Skills Development

The activities in this section support practitioners to develop universal skills for adopting a restorative approach in any setting. The first activity challenges learners to reframe how they think about the source and motivations for behaviors that have caused harm. The second activity helps learners fine-tune skills that help others feel heard and understood. The third activity inspires creativity for those seeking to generate more varied and meaningful ideas for reparative actions.

Needs and Feelings Iceberg

Objective
Participants will develop understanding about how unmet needs are often at the root of challenging behaviors.

Materials
- A slide with a visual of an iceberg with sections labeled behavior, feelings, and needs (see example). You will be adding text to the slide during the activity, so keep it as a PowerPoint or Google slide that you can screen share and edit (don't convert it to a pdf). You can download materials for this activity at restorativeteachingtools.com.
- List of feelings and list of needs provided on Marshall Rosenberg's Non-Violent Communication website (GROK cards is another product we recommend).

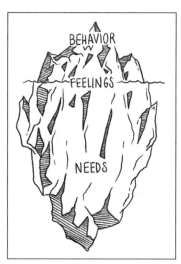

Instructions

Begin by explaining the visual of the iceberg model. For example,

- *What we can see is a person's behavior, so that is above waterline.*
- *Feelings are placed at the waterline because sometimes we can see the feelings a person may be experiencing, and sometimes we cannot.*
- *What we often can't see are the person's unmet needs that are ultimately driving the behavior. These are placed below the surface.*

When we learn to see challenging or problematic behavior through the lens of understanding the need that behavior is seeking to address, we become more empathetic and effective restorative practitioners. We become better able to support a process of identifying a pro-social way for those needs to be recognized and met, thereby addressing the root cause (the need) instead of the symptom (the behavior).

After explaining the iceberg visual, share an example case study of a problematic behavior and enough information about the person demonstrating the behavior for the group to be able to put themselves in that person's shoes and consider which feelings and needs may be at the root of the behavior.

We recommend you use an example case study from your context that is relevant to your community of learners (whether that is a community justice program, a school, a university, a workplace, or some other space). We are including one sample case study below from a school context.

Example Scenario

On a class trip, Alex and Marty sat in the back of the bus talking and laughing. Both boys were juniors who played on the varsity basketball team. They talked about the game the night before, assessing how they and others had played and commenting on why their team had lost so badly. A few of their classmates, some of them players, listened to Alex's and Marty's banter. Alex was proud of playing varsity and had invited his family to a game for the first time. After the game, his dad had made an offhand comment about Alex always playing on losing teams, leading Alex to feel insecure and frustrated.

Their joking crossed a line when Alex announced loudly that if Marty hadn't missed so many key shots, they might have won the game. As the team captain, Marty was already feeling troubled about this loss and the previous two games they had also lost. The coach had been putting a lot of pressure on him, telling him to step up and pull the team out of their losing streak. The coach's intensity was messing with his game. From his perspective, he had missed too many shots, and felt embarrassed about it. His new girlfriend had been at the game and he hadn't done anything to show her his skills on the court. This jab from Alex made Marty's blood boil and pushed him over the edge. He couldn't believe his own teammate was saying this kind of stuff, and within earshot of their friends. Marty told Alex to shut up and Alex laughed and muttered, "It hurts 'cause you know it's true."

At a rest stop, the students were told they could get off the bus to use the restroom. Marty waited until they were walking into the restroom and out of view of their teachers. He grabbed Alex by the shoulder, spun him around, and punched him hard in the stomach. Reeling, Alex struck back and knocked Marty to the ground. A few of their friends jumped in to separate them, just as a teacher walked around the corner to find Marty on the ground and Alex standing over him, yelling obscenities.

Both Alex and Marty took responsibility for their actions and agreed to participate in a restorative justice process that you will facilitate. You have some judgments about the boys and assumptions about why they would act this way, especially on a class trip. Before facilitating, you decide to pause and take some guesses about the possible feelings and needs at play that influenced the boys' behavior.

After sharing the case study, divide the group into two smaller groups and assign one group to reflect on feelings and needs that might be at the root of Alex's behavior, and one group to reflect on Marty's feelings and needs that might be driving his behavior. Give each group the lists of feelings and needs and a copy of the editable iceberg image slide and ask them to identify which feelings and needs may be relevant to the behaviors referenced in the case and to make a list. They will write what they come up with into the iceberg slide. Then, bring the full group back together. Ask each group to share the feelings and needs they identified while screensharing their iceberg visual.

It is important to remind learners that until they have a safe and respectful way to communicate directly with someone about their behavior, they are simply taking educated guesses about the feelings and needs at the root of that behavior. Encourage learners to remain curious. Remind them that the purpose of this hypothetical reflection is to move away from making quick, reactive assumptions about someone's behavior, and instead to broaden our thinking to become more empathetic and curious about what is driving that behavior.

This activity asks participants to suspend initial assumptions and judgments about someone's behavior by reframing the behavior through the lens of unmet needs. This helps build empathy and expand our understanding of the relationship between needs, feelings, and behavior, but in an actual restorative process, we would want to understand the feelings and needs at the root of the behavior by asking skillful, open-ended questions with a spirit of curiosity. Facilitate a conversation about how to do that with the group by posing the following two questions and creating a list of responses:

- What open-ended questions might you ask in a conversation with the person demonstrating this behavior in order to surface the feelings they were experiencing?
- What open-ended questions might you ask in a conversation with the person demonstrating this behavior in order to understand the unmet needs that may be at the root of their behavior?

You can bring embodiment into this activity by asking the groups to think about how to physically represent (through movement, physical gestures, facial expressions, etc.) the feelings and needs they think are related to the behavior. When the groups come back together, ask a few representatives from each group to demonstrate, through embodied expression, the feelings and needs they came up with. They may need to stand up and away from their camera for their full expression to be visible. Ask the other group to guess what feelings and needs are being acted out and to reflect on what they are seeing. Facilitate a mini-debrief about picking up on nonverbal communication in restorative processes.

Debrief

- How has this activity changed your perception of other people's behavior?
- How does an understanding of needs change your thoughts about possible reparative agreements that come out of a restorative justice process?
- How will this understanding of the relationship between needs and behaviors influence you moving forward?

Lesson

The behaviors we can see are just the tip of the iceberg. In order to develop restorative ways to explore behavior and build connection, we need to pause and practice considering the feelings and unmet needs that are at the root of those behaviors. From there we can work collaboratively to address them in a supportive, strengths-based way.

Instructions for In-Person Adaptation

If you are facilitating this activity in a small space, share the iceberg on slides or poster paper that you can write on. The feelings and needs can be written directly onto the iceberg, or you can have participants write each word on a Post-it or piece of paper and stick it to the large iceberg. If you have adequate space, we recommend adding a kinesthetic element by constructing a large version of the iceberg visual on the floor that participants can engage with. Or go outside and turn a playground structure into an iceberg!

"What I hear you saying is . . ."

Objective

This activity helps participants fine-tune their active listening skills by developing understanding of and practicing specific types of responses to the speaker. Participants will become familiar with the nuanced differences between reflective statements, affirmations, validations, and reframes.

It is important that you are familiar with and have practiced using each of these four strategies before leading this activity. Additionally, this is an activity for seasoned restorative practitioners to develop advanced skills. It will work most effectively with a community of learners that has already built relationships and has some degree of shared experiences with restorative work.

Materials

- Sets of flash cards with the following words on them, one word per card: Affirmation, Validation, Reflection, Reframe. These can be made simply with small pieces of paper or sticky notes and a pen. Each participant will need a set.
- Shared document (such as a Google doc) with three to eight short statements (numbered). It will make the most sense if you choose statements that you have actually heard or encountered in your community while engaging in restorative processes.

Instructions

First, you will need to familiarize yourself with the definitions of each of these strategies, as well as when and how to use each one:

> **Affirmation**: Emphasizes the implicit strength and/or effort in the speaker's statement. Builds self-efficacy and confidence.
>
> **Validation**: Reinforces that the speaker's experience or feelings make sense. Communicates empathy.
>
> **Reflection**: Synthesizes and repeats back the main points, feelings, or needs shared by the speaker. Allows the listener to check out their understanding of what was said.
>
> **Reframe**: A type of reflection that refocuses or redirects the emphasis of the speaker's statement. Defuses tension and re-contextualizes the topic.

Present a basic introduction to each of these strategies, with emphasis on the "why" (their purpose/ intended goal) and the "how" (their basic formula).

Divide learners into groups of two or three. Groups of three can be helpful because the third person can weigh in as a coach, giving additional ideas and perspective. In the chat, share a link to the shared document with the statements.

Give the following instructions to the full group:

> *In a moment, I will send you into breakout rooms in groups of three. You will be using the shared document with statements (link in the chat) and your flash cards with the four strategies (Affirmation, Validation, Reflection, Reframe). Person A will*

pick a statement from the document and read it out loud. Person B will select (without looking) a strategy card from their deck. Person B will then craft a response to the statement using that strategy. Person A listens to Person B's response, then continues in natural conversation. This is an important step as some learning will occur when learners observe how Person A responds to each strategy. Person C will listen and provide support and feedback as needed. Next, switch roles and repeat the process until all three group members have had at least one opportunity to come up with an affirmation, validation, reflection, or reframe.

It can be helpful to ask Person B to write down their response so that it is recorded and can be shared back during the debrief.

What follows is an example based on a harmed person saying "I think what he (responsible person) really needs is boot camp. When I was his age, I enlisted. We had to run for miles holding our rifles over our heads until we got sick. That will make him think differently about doing anything like this again."

- **Reflection:** It sounds like you are feeling frustrated and have some ideas about how (responsible person) could learn from this, based on your experience.
- **Validation:** I can understand that from your experience in the military, physical exertion is one way to create discipline.
- **Affirmation:** I hear that you have grown through physical discipline and perseverance

and believe that others need to learn the same way.

- **Reframe:** You have already thought about what might help (responsible person) learn from this incident. Let's brainstorm some more options. We're looking for ideas that help (responsible person) use their strengths to repair harmed relationships.

Provide a set amount of time for the breakout rooms (at least fifteen minutes). At the end of the time, bring the whole group together for the debrief.

For advanced practitioners looking to up-level their skills via more vulnerability and risk-taking, you can invite an additional phase of practice. In this phase, instead of utilizing the pre-written statements, participants will utilize personal experiences or beliefs that feel risky to share. For example, Person A could share a past choice that they regret, or state a controversial belief that they believe Person B may or may not agree with. Person B will still pull a strategy flash card and practice responding to Person A with that particular response. Note, this level of practice should only be introduced to groups of learners who have established trust and group norms for how to engage respectfully in the learning process.

Consider introducing an additional challenge by asking learners to practice each strategy without using the terms "It sounds like" and "What I hear you saying is," which often get overused.

Additional Example Statements

Feel free to use these examples at first, but keep in mind that your learners will benefit by utilizing examples that are derived from specific scenarios and statements from your community.

Example 1) Youth responsible person about their reparative contract: "I don't think I can manage this. I feel bad about what happened and I want to make things right, but I'm a failure. I just dropped out of school. I've never completed anything."

Example 2) Parent whose child has committed a crime: "I'm ready to give up on her. I've worked hard to get her the stable life I never had, but she's a lost cause. I've tried everything, even parenting classes. Nothing works."

Example 3) Harmed person about their neighbors: "I'm okay with this process going forward, but I'll never trust them again. I used to think we had something in common, we had some good chats and even threw a block party one summer. But now they think they can do whatever they want and just get a little slap on the wrist? I hope they learn something from this, but it seems like punishment is what really makes people think twice."

Example 4) Youth referred to restorative justice after a fight at school: "He had it coming. I tried to tell him, 'Just keep your distance, man.' He didn't listen. I guess I should've been the bigger person and walked away, but you know, I have a reputation to keep."

Example 5) Person taking responsibility for keying someone's car: "I am a terrible person. How could I have done this, and in front of my kids? I have been trying so hard to hold it all together and keep a smile on my face, but my life has gone off the rails. I want to be a good parent. This just isn't me."

Example 6) Youth taking responsibility for shoplifting: "I know I shouldn't have stolen these headphones. I figured it didn't really matter. These huge corporations, they aren't going to suffer from one little missing thing. It's like a drop in the bucket to them. But whatever, rules are rules."

Example 7) Harmed person: "You're not expecting me to forgive him, are you? I've been thinking about this a lot, and I know I don't want him to go to court. But I know this guy. He's got issues and he'll never change. This restorative process sounds pretty good, but I don't know if it will work on someone like him."

Debrief

- When you were the person listening and responding (Person B), which strategies were easier to apply when coming up with your response statement? Which were more challenging? What did you notice about the differences?
- When you were the speaker (Person A), how did the different strategies affect you and your relationship to the statement or scenario? How did they affect your connection with Person B?

Lesson

By becoming more intentional about how we listen for others' feelings, needs, strengths, and experiences, and deliberately choosing how we respond, we can offer a more empathetic connection with a harmed or responsible person (and others), and avoid habitual responses stemming from our opinions and biases. Developing a nuanced understanding of how to use these responses and their impacts enables us to choose how we listen and engage more effectively.

Recognize that as restorative practitioners, we will often hear others describe beliefs or behaviors that we don't relate to or agree with. Furthermore, the speaker may be struggling with shame, humiliation, and other difficult emotions surrounding their actions. In order to support the speaker's own self-determination and agency, it's important that we strive to avoid value judgments or evaluations of the speaker's choices in our responses. One way to do this is to listen carefully for the experiences, strengths, needs, and feelings that underlie those beliefs, behaviors, and choices.

At other times, someone may use language or share a view that is oppressive or harmful to others. In that case, be sure that your response validates or reflects the emotion they may be experiencing, but not the harmful view or belief. After building connection, find ways to name and address the harmful statement.

Out of the Box

Objective
Students will practice brainstorming and finalizing creative, strengths-based agreement items that are SMART (Specific, Measurable, Achievable, Related to repairing harm, and Timely) for restorative justice processes.

Materials
- A mock restorative justice case scenario
- A description of the responsible person's strengths and interests

To make this game fun and manageable online, you need a minimum of nine participants (in addition to the facilitators) and a maximum of twenty-five. This game is easier to lead with a co-facilitator. One facilitator leads the game, the other acts as the "judge."

Instructions
First, explain to the whole group that you will be dividing participants into teams (three to five people per team depending on group size) and sending each team into their own breakout room.

Give the following instructions:

I am going to share a case scenario and the responsible person's strengths. Each team will work together to write three agreement items that are creative, strengths-based, and SMART (Specific, Measurable, Achievable, Related to repairing the harm, and Timely) that could potentially be used in a restorative agreement to repair harm.

79

Here is the catch: all agreement items must be "out of the box" ideas, meaning they cannot be any one of the three most common agreement items (for example, apology letter, poster, and volunteer service hours).

Imagine that all the members of your team are standing in a box together. Your goal is to get all members of your team "out of the box" by coming up with creative, SMART agreement item ideas. After ten minutes, I will bring all teams back into the main meeting space for Round 1. I will call on each group to read one idea at a time, i.e. Team A reads one idea, then Team B reads one idea, then Team C, etc. The other teams must pause and listen. The idea must be read in one continuous statement (as it would be written in a restorative agreement) and clearly have all the elements of SMART.

I (or the "judge" if you have a co-facilitator) will respond to each agreement item after it is read and will determine if it has met all the SMART criteria. If I accept the item, the person who voiced that item will symbolically step "out of the box" by turning off their video and muting themselves. They are now a silent observer, and can no longer make suggestions. If I reject the item, you can choose to continue working on it when I send you back into breakout rooms, but another group can also "steal" that idea and try to make it fit the criteria. The first team to get all members "out of the box" wins.

Adjust the "three most common agreement items" according to your context. If the community you are working with tends to overly rely on certain agreement items, you can make those part of "the box" and require participants to come up with different creative ideas.

After the teams have read all three of their ideas in Round 1 and you (or the "judge") have accepted or rejected each idea, send the teams back into their breakout rooms to continue working on additional SMART, out of the box agreement items. Reduce the amount of time they have to eight or six minutes (you can always visit the breakout rooms to see how each team is doing time-wise), then bring them back together to the main space for Round 2. Have the teams share back their ideas, one by one, as you did in Round 1 (switch up the sharing order so a different team starts each round). Continue this process until one team gets all team members "out of the box," which will look like all those team members having their video off and sound muted. Announce the winning team, and they can turn on their cameras to celebrate!

The facilitator needs to be prepared to listen to each proposed agreement item to determine in the moment if it fits all criteria. Depending on group size, this game may require a fair amount of time to complete. Plan for at least forty-five minutes to play and fifteen minutes to debrief. If you don't have enough time to run the game through completion, pause it with enough time to synthesize learning and hold the debrief.

This game can be a little wild and chaotic at first, and that's part of the fun! The facilitator must orchestrate the game, the judging of ideas, and indicate which team has the floor, making sure that teams are taking turns. This requires a facilitator who is ready to think on their feet and manage a lot of activity. Recruit a good co-facilitator to help you facilitate the first time, don't take yourself too seriously, and don't give up!

Debrief

- Ask the last person who was left "in the box": How was it different for you to brainstorm ideas with a big group versus alone?
- Ask everyone: How did your group work together to create agreement ideas? What got your creativity going? How was your brainstorming affected by removing the three most common agreement items?

Lesson

When we think outside the box and brainstorm together, we are able to come up with more varied and creative ideas to repair harms. Students practice and learn the importance of making an agreement idea SMART.

Instructions for In-Person Adaption

Instructions for playing this game in person can be found in *The Little Book of Restorative Teaching Tools*.

Chapter 7
Games and Activities for Understanding and Addressing Structural Injustices

> "Restorative justice risks losing relevance if we, as practitioners, do not become more skillful at identifying, navigating, and transforming racial harm. . . . Given the nation's changing demographics and persistent, if not deepening, racial disparities, a restorative justice approach that ignores these inequities will be perceived as uninformed and uncaring, if not irrelevant and racist."
> —Fania Davis, *The Little Book of Race and Restorative Justice*

Building understanding and accountability around racism and structural injustices is a critical element in all restorative justice education. Practitioners are responsible for understanding racism and other forms of oppression, and how they can be perpetuated in restorative justice and society more broadly. This requires deliberate attention and reflection on racism and its impacts as it exists culturally, institutionally, interpersonally, and intrapersonally. The activities in this section offer a few ways to develop awareness about racism and structural injustices within a restorative justice framework. They will be most effective when used as a component of a more comprehensive curriculum of racial justice education.

Your own preparation and self-reflection as a facilitator are crucial. We (the authors) are both white women who have experienced privilege in many ways throughout our lives. Facilitating activities focused on race and white privilege requires our ongoing learning and self-reflection as we strive to hold supportive and challenging learning spaces. We are on an unending journey of unlearning, learning, practicing accountability to own the harm we cause, and working to avoid causing harm moving forward. We encourage you to ask a trusted peer to help you co-facilitate so that you can debrief the activity and support each other's reflections and learning.

The first activity is intended for restorative justice practitioners who can apply their direct experience with restorative justice casework to the exercise. Learners will have a more meaningful and focused discussion if they already have established relationships and have worked through challenging topics that surface differing viewpoints. The second activity prompts learners to apply a restorative justice lens to historical events, which both strengthens understanding of restorative principles and reframes our understanding of historical events from a one-sided view to a multi-perspective view emphasizing responsibility, impacts, and reparations. The third activity guides learners to engage with a young adult novel about restorative justice by exploring questions of equity, social determinants of health, and resiliency in the characters' lives.

It is important to assess the readiness level of learners before implementing these activities and to have laid the groundwork for a supportive learning environment that will encourage vulnerability, open-mindedness, and self-reflection. If you are working with a group of learners who are primarily white, consider scaffolding their readiness to participate in these activities by engaging with anti-racism resources prior to facilitating these activities. For white facilitators, it is critically important that you have done your own self-reflective work on these themes so that you can show up with clarity, compassion, and accountability as you navigate these discussions.

As participants in the restorative movement, we have an implicit responsibility to work to dismantle oppressive and punitive systems. It is our hope that these activities will help spark dialogue that allows us to identify unforeseen possibilities that lead to committed and sustained justice and healing.

Identifying, Navigating & Transforming Racial Harm

Objective

Participants will recognize that restorative justice exists within and is informed by racist structures, institutions, and individual bias. Participants will discuss the role and impacts of interpersonal, institutional, and systemic racism in a given crime or conflict scenario and will engage in honest discussions about racism in their communities and lives. Participants' understanding of their responsibility as restorative justice practitioners will expand as they seek to address the root causes that perpetuate harm and inequity.

Materials

- Pre-reading for participants: Chapter 3, from Fania Davis's *The Little Book of Race and Restorative Justice: Black Lives, Healing, and US Social Transformation* (Skyhorse, 2019).
- Copies of pages 32–34, including Figure 1 (3 Types of Racism), from Davis's *The Little Book of Race and Restorative Justice.*

86

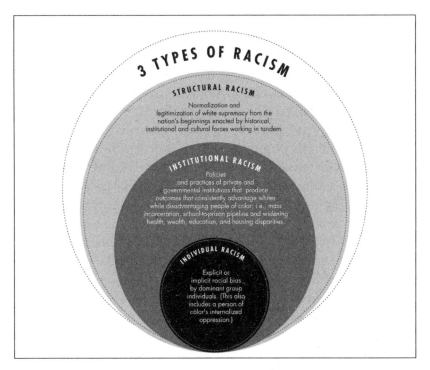

Three types of racism, from Fania Davis's *Little Book of Race and Restorative Justice.*

Instructions

Prior to the activity, ask participants to read Chapter 3 "Integrating Racial Justice and Restorative Justice" of Fania Davis's *The Little Book of Race and Restorative Justice.* Reading the whole book is strongly encouraged, but not required for this activity.

Review Davis's model of Three Types of Racism with learners and explain that this activity is designed to deepen your understanding of the three types of racism by analyzing a real-life case through the lens of each form of racism. We have provided one case example below. This activity will be most relevant if you select a case that has been referred to restorative justice in your community and involves at least one person who identifies as BIPOC. Or, you could select a current event to analyze. If working with a current event, frame the activity through the lens of "What if this were referred to restorative justice?"

Read the case example out loud before dividing participants into three groups of three to four people each. Assign each group a type of racism: structural, institutional, or individual. Each group is responsible for examining how that one type of racism is impacting the people in the case. If you are working with a group that is larger than fifteen people, consider utilizing two different case studies to keep group size small.

Ask each group to ensure every person has a chance to speak. Give the groups at least ten minutes for open discussion, then shift their focus toward the questions listed below. Provide twenty-five minutes for the groups to work through questions 1 through 4. Ask the groups to assign one scribe, or decide as a group how they will track and share back their discussion with the larger group. Send each group into a separate breakout room. Let them know how much time they will have in the breakout rooms.

Acknowledge that this is an exercise. Because the individuals involved in the case are not in the room, most of what is discussed will be hypothetical. The goal is to expand your thinking about the case and to better understand the three types of racism by applying them to an incident from your community.

When time is up, bring everyone back together. Ask each group to report back on the following questions.

1. How is the type of racism your group was assigned evident in this case? What are the impacts? Name two or three ways.
2. How might a facilitator ask questions to surface how this form of racism is a force at play in this case?
3. What could repair look like for the impacts of this type of racism?

After all three groups have shared, pose this question to all participants: In what ways have the overlap or interplay of the three forms of racism influenced this incident?

Facilitator Notes

1. Reinforce learners' approaching this activity with a spirit of curiosity. Be prepared to reframe shaming or blaming comments that can derail learning.
2. Validate expressions of sincere responsibility-taking and work to keep the group from minimizing or abdicating responsibility. Look out for signs of students' justifying indicators of racism for the sake of avoiding their own discomfort.
3. Be ready to intervene if the group begins to lean on BIPOC participants in the group to educate others about the realities of racism and its impacts. Based on your relationship with this group of learners, you could check in with these individuals in advance of the activity to ask them if and how they would like to participate.

Online Learning Tip

It can be more difficult to speak up and address a difficult moment online than it is in person. Due to the audio functions and lag times on virtual platforms, you may actually need to interrupt in order to intervene when you believe harm may occur. This may be uncomfortable for you and others, and it's critical that you are prepared for this discomfort. It may be useful to introduce a break to give everyone a pause, then address the difficult experience following the break. Or, you may need to address a harmful comment outside the training session itself. It is essential to be transparent and follow through with difficult conversations in order to maintain a respectful, brave, and restorative learning environment.

Example Case

Wanda and Katie are first-year college students and members of a competitive debate team. Wanda is Black and is a first-generation college student from Chicago. Katie is white and her parents met at the college she and Wanda attend. They practice three days a week for debate, are in a sociology class together, and frequently attend the same parties, but they aren't close friends.

Wanda has been feeling increasingly frustrated by the lack of diversity in the student body and the overrepresentation of white voices in the sociology curriculum. In particular, her Intro to Sociology class is taught by a white female professor and the syllabus doesn't include any work by BIPOC authors or researchers. When Wanda raised the issue with the professor, she responded that her syllabus was built on the seminal texts in the field because it was a foundations course and all those scholars just "happen to be white."

At the end of debate practice one day, Katie approached Wanda. "Are you going to the party tonight?" she asked. "I think so," said Wanda. "Your hair is so beautiful, you should wear it like this tonight," said Katie, grabbing one of Wanda's braids and rubbing it between her fingers. "I'm so jealous!" Then Katie turned and walked away.

Wanda was fuming as she left, feeling like every part of her college experience was weighing on her all at the same time. No one seemed to care about these countless microaggressions, and no one seemed to listen, not even her family. She walked out of the building and through the parking lot where she saw Katie's car. Without thinking, she pulled out her keys, and dragged one key down the side of Katie's car.

The security cameras in the parking lot recorded what Wanda did. She admitted to keying the car when confronted by campus security and she was referred to the university restorative justice program.

Debrief

- How did this exploration of the three types of racism change your view of this case?
- How will the awareness you gained in this activity inform your facilitation or

participation in future restorative justice cases?

* How did this activity affect your understanding of your own identity and community?

Lesson

As restorative justice practitioners, we have a responsibility to develop an expansive view of every case to understand how structural and institutional forces are at play, in addition to the individual and interpersonal dynamics. As a movement, restorative justice runs the risk of inadvertently perpetuating the harms of systems it seeks to transform if racial justice is not central in our work.

Instructions for In-Person Adaptation

When you bring the group back together, have the participants stand in concentric circles that reflect Davis's model of the Three Types of Racism as they share out from their small group discussions. This physical arrangement will reinforce how individual racism exists within a context of institutional racism, which is nested within structural racism.

Viewing History through a Restorative Lens

Objective

Learners will reflect on a historical or current event through a restorative lens. They will consider different perspectives, identify who was impacted, and think critically about what needs to happen now to begin to repair the harm caused to the greatest extent possible. These instructions use the example of the War on Drugs, supporting learners to better understand the structural and systemic racism of the criminal legal system in the United States, but this activity can be used to examine any historical or current event.

Materials

- Pre-reading: "The Lockdown" chapter from Michelle Alexander's *The New Jim Crow: Mass Incarceration in the Age of Colorblindness* (The New Press, 2012).
- A shared document (such as a Google doc) with a template that has two columns, one for recording harms or impacts, and one for recording ideas for repair.
- Optional pre-reading/watching: First-person accounts of the War on Drugs from, for example, the website for Families Against Mandatory Minimums (FAMM), which has a collection of stories from people incarcerated for drug offenses and their families. Or, Ronald Reagan's speech to the nation on the campaign against drug abuse (September 14, 1986), which is available on YouTube.

To learn about the War on Drugs in a larger context of historical and present-day violence against Black people and other People of Color, watch Ava DuVernay's film, *13th*.

Instructions

Before beginning the activity, ask participants to read "The Lockdown," a chapter from Michelle Alexander's *The New Jim Crow* (and/or some first-person accounts by those impacted by the War on Drugs, such as those listed above).

Explain that for this activity, the group will be looking at a historical event (in this case, the War on Drugs) and how it has shaped the present through a restorative lens. Learners will be endeavoring to understand what happened from different perspectives of people involved, who was impacted and how, and what might happen to begin to repair the harm caused.

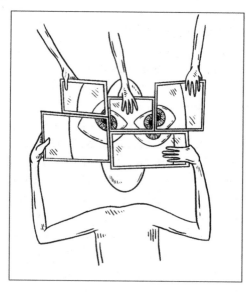

Question 1: What happened?

The first question to consider is "What happened?" Explain that in a restorative process, we have the opportunity to hear what happened from the perspective of the people directly involved in an incident. We will replicate that experience in this activity by putting ourselves in the shoes of a few different parties related to the War on Drugs.

Divide the group into smaller groups depending on how many perspectives you would like to explore. Send each small group into their own breakout room. Some possible perspectives to use for the War on Drugs:

- A person incarcerated for a drug offense
- The family of someone incarcerated for a drug offense
- Community members or groups with different racial and ethnic identities, i.e. a Black family, a white family, an immigrant family (to make it most locally relevant, choose racial groups represented in your community in addition to those most directly involved)
- A police officer
- A judge
- A teacher or social worker
- Former President Ronald Reagan

Ask each group to consider how their assigned individual or group might answer the question "What happened?" Give them ten minutes to discuss and then close the breakout rooms to reconvene as a large group. Ask each group to report back with a two-minute summary to the larger group. Take a few minutes to debrief the experience of hearing multiple perspectives. Ask:

- How were you affected by hearing different perspectives side by side?
- How did it change your view of the issue?

Question 2: Who has been affected and how?

Move on to the second restorative question "Who has been affected and how?" Pose this question to the entire group (no breakout rooms this time) and start a list titled "Impacted People" that everyone can see, utilizing the screenshare function, a shared document, or the chat. Record all the names of impacted people and groups learners come up with. Acknowledge that some of their ideas will be purely hypothetical and it is okay to make guesses during this activity. Remind learners to consider ripple effects as they name impacted parties. It will be helpful if you brainstorm a diverse list of impacted people/groups prior to facilitating the activity so that you can support participants by naming people they left out.

Encourage everyone to contribute to this brainstorm. After the group has brainstormed a list of impacted people/groups, divide them into new small groups (three to four people in each group) and assign one impacted person/group to each small group. You may also invite participants to choose the impacted person/group they would like to work with.

Invite the small groups to reflect on how the impacted person they were assigned (or chose) was affected. Ask them to be specific, go deep, and bring a spirit of curiosity to the dialogue. It will be helpful for each group to assign one person as the notetaker. Provide the groups with the shared document template that has two columns, one for recording harms or impacts, and one for recording ideas for repair. The notetaker will be responsible for typing the group's ideas into the document so they can be shared when the groups return from the breakout rooms.

Move the small groups into breakout rooms. Give them at least ten minutes to discuss the impacts before bringing them back together. When you bring everyone back together, ask each small group to screenshare their document and talk about the harms or impacts they identified.

After each group has shared, send them back into breakout rooms with the third question.

Question 3: What could be done to repair the harms and impacts we identified?

Ask each group to brainstorm what could be done now to begin to repair the harms their impacted person or group has experienced. Ask them to consider who is responsible to repair that harm. Remind students that this is unlike many restorative justice repair agreements, which typically occur within an established timeframe of a few months. In circumstances involving prolonged harms, reparations require sustained commitments and change, rather than one-time acts. Discuss the generational trauma caused by institutionalized racism and its impacts.

Prioritize using a restorative lens by designing reparations that are actionable and specifically relate to harms, to the greatest degree possible. Be creative and think outside the box. For example, how might reparative actions interact with the arts and elevate diverse cultural practices that promote holistic healing and community resilience? Ask the notetaker to record all ideas in the same template, in the repair column. Give the small groups fifteen to twenty minutes in breakout rooms to discuss these questions.

Close the breakout rooms to bring the small groups back together. Ask each group to screenshare their document and talk about what reparative actions they brainstormed, and who would be responsible for those actions. After each group has spoken, ask the large group:

- What can we as individuals do to work to repair the harms caused by the War on Drugs?
- What can we do as a community?

Record responses to these questions in another list that all participants can see. Commit to sharing these lists with all participants via email after the end of the training or class.

We also recommend using this activity to learn about and develop reparative action ideas for historic and ongoing harms caused to Native peoples. Begin by doing research about the Native peoples who inhabit or inhabited the place where you live. You can utilize https://native-land.ca/ as an initial reference point. Search for information about a specific historical event that caused harm to those people, such as an incident of violence, boarding schools, forced labor, separation of families, violation of treaties, or widespread disease introduced by colonizers. Study this event from several sources if possible so you can help guide learners through the activity. Use the three questions as directed in the activity instructions. When debriefing, encourage learners to continue their research to learn about land back movements and other reparative actions that are underway. Ask learners how they might be able to support these movements in large and small ways.

Debrief

- What did you learn by looking at a historical event that has shaped the current state of the criminal legal system through a restorative lens? (Edit this question as necessary if the historical event is not connected to the criminal legal system.)
- How did it affect your perspective? What surprised you?
- How will learning through this lens influence your actions moving forward?

Lesson

The restorative philosophy and process provide a helpful and insightful framework to view historical and current events. By taking the time to understand what happened and explore impacts from diverse perspectives, we begin to interrupt complacent acceptance of the past and activate awareness and accountability. As restorative practitioners committed to racial justice, we must develop our own sense of agency to make reparations through our beliefs, words, and actions.

Play the Game

Objective

Play the Game by Charlene Allen is a novel that explores restorative justice and the need for restorative responses to incidents of interpersonal harm, community violence, and larger structural injustices. This activity is designed as a companion to the novel to invite learners to step into the shoes of different characters and develop an understanding of structural and racial injustices and how they impact the characters' lives. Participants will also develop an appreciation of the unique strengths and resilience that each character holds, and how the restorative justice processes in the book support each character's healing journey.

Materials
- Pre-reading: *Play the Game* by Charlene Allen (Katherine Tegen Books, 2023). (The first half is read before the first activty session and the second half is read in advance of the second activity session—see details below.)
- Slide template for this activity (found on www.restorativeteachingtools.com)

Instructions

This activity utilizes concepts from video games to explore several characters' experiences at specific points in the book. Learners will study one character and use the framework of a video game health bar to analyze the character's health or well-being, considering the impact of specific events and broader structural injustices on their lives. Learners will also use the framework of a video game inventory to consider the strengths and resiliency factors they possess.

This activity takes place over two classes or trainings, the first when learners have read approximately half the book and the second when they have completed the book. Prior to the first class or training, ask learners to have read through page 158 (the end of "The Devil's Daughter" chapter) of *Play the Game*.

Session 1 (pre-reading: through p. 158)

Start by explaining the concepts of a "health bar" and "inventory" as they are used in video games:

A "health bar" in video games is a meter that indicates a character's or avatar's health. This bar typically displays the amount of health a character has remaining, and as the character sustains injuries in the game, the health bar decreases. When the health bar is depleted, it often results in the character's death or failure in the game, depending on the game's mechanics. The health bar is a fundamental element in many video games, helping players monitor their character's well-being during gameplay.

An "inventory" in video games refers to the equipment bar or menu where players can access and manage various equipment, such as weapons, armor, and other resources that their in-game character possesses. The inventory menu allows players to equip, use, discard, or manage their items as needed to progress through the game. In this activity, we will be using the concept of an inventory to consider the specific strengths that a character has that can help them on their journey.

Divide the group into smaller groups of three to four people each. Each small group will be assigned one character and will be answering questions about that character's experience. Remind learners that they know more about some of these characters than others, and this activity will involve making some educated guesses in the interest of building their understanding of and empathy with the characters. We recommend assigning the following characters:

- VZ
- Jack
- Chela
- Diamond
- Junie
- Robbie

One person in each group will be editing a Google slide that has a template for displaying their character's "health bar" and "inventory." Health refers to their well-being, and inventory refers to their strengths and resources.

Each group will discuss their character's health and strengths. They will reflect these discussions by setting up their character's health bar and inventory on their slide to present to the large group. Provide the following questions to the small groups to guide their discussion:

1. How is the health and well-being of this character, on a scale from 1–10? On your slide, fill in the number of hearts to indicate their health level, with 10 being the healthiest. In your discussion, think beyond recent events to consider broader social determinants of health. Questions to consider when determining their health:
   a. What is the impact of Ed's murder on this character?
   b. How much social support do they have (from peers or adults)? Do they have people they trust, who have their back? Who?
   c. What is this character's experience related to their identity (race, gender, sexual orientation, etc.)?
   d. Consider other social determinants of health for this character in assessing their health and well-being, such as their income, education, employment, access to food, housing, and basic amenities, early childhood experiences, social inclusion and non-discrimination, access to affordable health services, exposure to violence, etc.

2. What strengths or resources does this character have? Write one strength per star to fill in your character's inventory of strengths. Possible sources of strength include: support from family and friends, individual talents, passions and interests,

103

access to help, purpose and drive, prosocial choices, positions of leadership and influence, knowledge and skills, etc. Try thinking outside the box and get creative to identify strengths.

Give the groups approximately fifteen to twenty-five minutes to work on their character's health bar and inventory of strengths.

Close the breakout rooms and bring everyone into the main meeting space. Ask each group to present their slide and their reasoning behind their character's health bar and inventory of strengths. After each group has presented, ask the following reflection questions.

- After doing this activity, how has your perspective of the story changed?
- Which character do you understand differently now? How has this activity influenced your understanding of that character?
- How has the activity changed your understanding of how identity and social conditions impact health? How does that understanding influence you as a restorative justice practitioner?
- How can you apply or relate this activity to real life?
- How does using the health and inventory framework affect how you think about yourself?

- How does this activity affect how you think about others (peers, clients, neighbors, colleagues)?

Prior to the second class or training, ask learners to have finished reading *Play the Game.*

Session 2 (pre-reading: p. 159 to end of book)

Ask learners to return to the same groups from the first class/training to consider the experiences of their assigned character again. Ask them to look at the slide where they previously assessed the health bar and inventory for their character and consider the restorative justice processes that took place in *Play the Game.* Provide the following questions to the small groups to guide their discussion.

1. How is this character's health and well-being at the end of the book compared to when we last considered it?
2. What was the impact of the restorative justice process on this character? What changed for them as a result of the restorative justice experience?
3. What was the impact of restorative justice on their health and well-being? What specifically accounts for this impact?

Ask the groups to update their character's health bar and inventory based on their discussion.

Give the groups approximately fifteen minutes to do so.

Close the breakout rooms and bring everyone into the main meeting space. Ask each group to present their slide and their reasoning behind their character's updated health bar and inventory of strengths. After each group has presented, ask the following debrief questions.

Debrief

- How has returning to your character's "health bar" and "inventory" impacted your understanding of restorative justice?
- How can you apply or relate this activity to real life?

Lesson

There are many influences affecting a person's experience, choices, and actions at any given time. Some of those influences we see, some we might be able to take guesses about, and others we will never fully understand. It's important to recognize that every person does not have equal access to rights and opportunities due to personal, societal, and structural conditions. We can engage with the characters in this story to make educated guesses about the factors and forces at play in their lives, and begin to understand how equity impacts their health and agency. We can also see how restorative justice contributes to healing and change on individual and collective levels.

Acknowledgments

We wish to express gratitude to our family members, friends, colleagues, and the many folks we have grown and learned with while doing restorative work. On a few occasions over the past four years, we have invited participants in our online workshops to co-create new activities with us. We want to recognize their collaboration as they shared learning needs and ideas. Several individuals made significant contributions that have helped this book take shape. Coco (Colleen) McGuire offered her artistic talents again to provide imaginative illustrations that bring our activities to life. We will forever admire Coco's ability to translate words to images after only hearing an activity described once. We appreciate our editor Barb Toews for believing in the importance of a second volume of restorative teaching tools, and helping us fine-tune our manuscript. Charlene Allen has gifted the restorative field with such an impactful resource through her book *Play the Game,* which we both found to be a page-turner! Thank you, Charlene, for allowing us to develop an activity to accompany your work and for your helpful feedback. We are grateful to Kathy Zaleski and Matt Hofmeister, two of our cherished friends, for sharing inspiration and wisdom from their experiences as restorative practitioners in schools.

We offer gratitude and respect to the global Indigenous traditions from which modern day restorative justice practices grew and continue to grow. We are thankful for the countless restorative practitioners and advocates who energize and shape the movement with their creativity and passion, and for the many people who have guided us in our own learning journeys.

We give thanks to the Colorado sun, mountains, and rivers that nourish us. We celebrate the joy of relationships with people and places that fuel us with love and hope.

About the Authors

Kathleen McGoey (she/her) is a trainer and facilitator of restorative justice practices and conflict transformation. With a background leading restorative justice implementation in communities and schools, she currently supports cities, workplaces, and families to utilize restorative approaches to address incidents of harm. This is Kathleen's third publication since completing an MA in International Peace and Conflict Studies at the University of Innsbruck, Austria. She lives in Colorado.

Lindsey Pointer (she/her) is an Assistant Professor at Vermont Law and Graduate School and Principal Investigator for the National Center on Restorative Justice. In addition to *The Little Book of Restorative Teaching Tools* (2020), Lindsey is the author of *The Restorative Justice Ritual* (2021) and *Wally and Freya* (2022), a children's picture book about restorative justice. Lindsey has a PhD in Restorative Justice from Victoria University of Wellington in New Zealand and is a former Fulbright and Rotary Global Grant recipient. She lives in Colorado.